Text copyright © Nai

Legal and Disclaimer

The information contained in this book and its contents is not designed to replace or take the place of any form of medical or professional advice; and is not meant to replace the need for independent medical, financial, legal or other professional advice or services, as may be required. The content and information in this book has been provided for educational and entertainment purposes only.

The content and information contained in this book has been compiled from sources deemed reliable, and it is accurate to the best of the author's knowledge, information and belief. However, the author cannot guarantee its accuracy and validity and cannot be held liable for any errors and/or omissions. Further, changes are periodically made to this book as and when needed. Where appropriate and/or necessary, you must consult a professional (including but not limited to your doctor, attorney, financial adviser or such other professional adviser) before using any of the suggested remedies, techniques or information in this book.

Upon using the contents and information contained in this book, you . agree to hold harmless the author from and against any damages, costs and expenses, including any legal fees potentially resulting from the application of any of the information provided by this book.

This disclaimer applies to any loss, damages or injury caused by the use and application, whether directly or indirectly, of any advice or information presented, whether for breach of contract, tort, negligence, personal injury, criminal intent or under any other cause of action.

You agree to accept all risks of using the information presented inside this book.

You agree that by continuing to read this book, where appropriate and/or necessary, you shall consult a professional (including but not limited to your doctor, attorney, or financial adviser or such other adviser as needed) before using any of the suggested remedies, techniques or information in this book.

ACKNOWLEDGEMENTS

I would like to acknowledge my loving husband for the support and encouragement that he gave me through the whole writing process to see this book complete. The advice he shared with me went a long way towards helping us come up with the contents of this book. I would like to thank the research team for researching deeply into the topic to give the best content. I thank you all from the bottom of my heart.

I dedicate this book to my loving husband for being a source of inspiration, motivation and strength. A true blessing in my life, and I thank God for you. Thank you ,Hubby.

Where Is the Off Button?

CHAPTER 4

4.1 FAQ

4.2 Sleeping Schedule

CONCLUSION

INTRODUCTION

We are usually all excited and anxious when there is a newborn on the way, but no one prepares us for what is coming. There are various challenges that, as a new parent, you will face along the way, but with proper knowledge and skills, you will go through them smoothly. Sleep is usually one of the major challenges that new parents and even experienced ones face with their children. This is because sleep patterns vary from one child to another.

Normally, you will face sleep challenges when your child is 4–6 weeks old. During this period they may sleep well during the day and become very active at night. As they grow, their sleeping patterns will also change. If your baby has regular patterns, it becomes easier for you to adapt and encourage desirable sleeping patterns. For parents with children whose patterns change regularly, it is necessary to set some common baseline for observing your child. This will help both you and your child have good sleep.

CHAPTER 1

1.1 Children's Sleeping Patterns

Newborns, when they are a few weeks old, do not know the difference between day and night. They normally sleep up to 16–18 hours a day. However, there are some variations in sleeping patterns as your child grows. Most parents enter panic mode when their child sleeps for longer hours or shorter than they expect.

Here are the sleeping patterns of children at various stages.

2–4 months: During this period your baby will start sleeping longer at night – six hours or more. Their stomach is growing, and it can accommodate more milk, preventing your child from waking up to feed every few minutes. Your baby will sleep around 15 hours a day when they are around three months, two-thirds of it being during the night.

5–7 months: During this period your baby's sleeping patterns are less stressful. At six months, your baby normally won't need to be fed or given their bottle during the night. At this age, they might take naps adding up to 3–4hours during the day and eight hours sleep during the night.

8–12 months: Your baby will be very active during the day, taking around two naps, and will sleep for around nine hours at night. By the time your child is celebrating their second birthday, they will likely be having a nap only once during the day.

They may indicate they are ready to sleep in several ways. These may include the baby rubbing their eyes, yawning, fussing, crying or looking away. Parents should be able to interpret their child's gestures when they are sleepy.

1.2 Healthy Sleeping Habits for a Child

All infants are at risk of sudden infant death syndrome (SIDS).It is more common in children between 1–4months but can affect infants up to 12months. Most SIDS deaths occur when a baby that is accustomed to sleeping on their back is put to bed on their tummy (unaccustomed tummy sleeping). It is estimated that one in five SIDS deaths occur when the baby is in the care of guardians who are not their parents. This can be reduced by the parents informing the guardians of the routine sleeping position of their baby.

Babies should eat appropriately before bed. Children who go to bed hungry or overfed usually have interrupted sleep due to stomach discomfort. A light meal before bed is recommended.

Regular exercise for your child: this does not mean you carry your child with you to the gym or cardio workout. Your child should be active and playful during the day to ease the metabolism and also improve their development. This will leave your child exhausted, and their sleep will be smooth throughout the night.

Maintain a consistent sleeping schedule for your child. They should have regular bedtimes and waking up times. Having a routine will allow the body to adapt and build sleep pressure in the body just before bed, making it easy for your child to sleep during their designated time.

While the baby is sleeping, make sure that their head remains uncovered to prevent them from suffocating themselves. This also includes placing them on a firm mattress and removing pillows, stuffed toys or waterbed.

Plan a quiet time before bed to help your child relax. This should be at least an hour before bedtime and take place in their bedroom.

Parents should also give their child a chance to learn how to fall asleep independently. Children who are three months old and healthy are recommended to learn how to fall asleep own their own. Starting this process during the early stages will help to prevent sleeping problems accelerating to the chronic stages.

Parents should encourage naps. Experts state that the better rested a child is, the easier it will be for them to sleep. It also encourages development in your baby's health.

CHAPTER 2

2.1 Interruptions During Sleep

All children wake up in the middle of the night, and those whose sleep has not been interrupted by certain factors will easily drift back to sleep. Sometimes you may not even realise they have been awake. If there is something that interrupts your child once in a while, those are the disturbances parents can deal with when they occur. But when a specific disturbance wakes your child every night, that calls for drastic measures to be taken. Some of these interruptions – and how to handle them – include

- *Sleep-disordered breathing (SDB)*:This term includes a wide spectrum of disorders that are a result of sleeping difficulties. Human beings spend 30% of their lives sleeping. Sleep disturbances often lead to bad health. They include loud breathing, interrupted breathing, snoring and trouble breathing during sleep. Sleep-disordered breathing can prevent oxygen reaching your child's brain and cause fatal health problems. SDB is closely associated with hyperactivity, night-time crying, night waking, attention problems and poor-quality sleep. Snoring is the most common SDB manifestation and can also be a symptom of sleep apnoea. It is important to see a physician when a child starts to snore, although it is important to note that not all children who snore have sleep apnoea.

- *Gastroesophageal Reflux (GER):* GER (stomach acid in the oesophagus, commonly known as heartburn) may cause frequent waking of children who suffer from it. It is also

11

- closely associated with other sleep interruptions such as sleep-disordered breathing, which can be fatal. Children who suffer from GER should not be given high-acidity food before bedtime. Heartburn is a common condition and can also be managed by buying anti-acid medicines. When heartburn increases to the extent that it causes disturbances in a child's life, it may be an indication of a more complex problem, and you should see a doctor.

- *Fear of being alone*: When your child wakes up and realises that they are alone, they may not go back to sleep. Parents should let their children learn to sleep by themselves. Each time they wake up and you go to sleep with them or hold them until they are asleep, you are reinforcing the fear in them. However, it is necessary to train them when they already fear being alone. Initially, leaving the light on may be a good way to start encouraging them not to be afraid. Communication is important in this aspect – children tend to trust their parents, and creating a mindset that there is nothing that can hurt them is important.

- *Nightmares*: Scary dreams are closely associated with REM sleep, which normally occurs when your child has been asleep for a couple of hours. Children are more likely to remember the nightmare when they wake up immediately from it. There are some aspects associated with triggers for nightmares, including traumatic events, anxiety, stress and medication that disorientates REM sleep. Children who have woken up from these bad dreams need to be reassured that everything is fine, that they are protected and that their dreams were not real. It may seem simple, but it goes a long way to reassuring your child of their safety and building their

12

confidence. When nightmares occur as a result of traumatic experiences, there is a need to see a child psychologist to help the child understand what is going on, and this is crucial to reassuring them that they are safe and will not get hurt. Immediately after they wake up from a nightmare it is important for an adult to be present to get them to sleep, and a crucial element in making them feel safe. An adult being present also helps to build trust between parents or guardians and the child.

- *Night terrors*: Just like nightmares, night terrors are disruptive, stressful and also cause night waking. The difference between a nightmare and night terrors is that your child may sleep walk during a night-terror, placing them at risk of injury or other, potentially fatal, accidents. Night terrors are more dangerous than nightmares in this regard and require a special attention. If a child sleepwalks at night, it is important to install special safety features that will ensure they will not get hurt. This includes making sure the room is safe, and closing stairways. The child should be taken to a physician to find out the cause and help eradicate them.

- *A full nappy*: This causes discomfort and can wake your child. The parent should change their baby's nappy before bedtime but after they are fed. A full nappy may cause nappy rash, which can keep the child awake at night due to the itchy feeling they experience.

- *Sleep onset associations*: Researchers state that children normally learn to relate falling asleep with certain kinds of stimulation, which may include the particular sleeping environment or parental soothing. These associations can be

13

very helpful for children, but if they become dependent on them, they fail to learn how to fall asleep on their own. Such sleep stimulation should stop at the age when children start learning how to do specific things on their own. When children become too dependent on stimulation, they never learn to fall asleep on their own and this can be a long-term problem.

- *Cold*: If your child wakes up every night because they are cold as a result of uncovering themselves, try tucking them into bed when they are already asleep.

- *Fear of the dark*: Many children are afraid of the dark, and this may cause your child to start crying if they wake up. Try plugging in a nightlight or letting them sleep with the lamp on. Do not switch it off after they are asleep, because they are likely to wake up in the middle of the night. Research states that children whose fears are ignored are more likely to suffer from emotional problems and nightmares. It is therefore vital that the parents actively teach their children how to overcome their fears.

- *Stress*: Children suffer from sleep interruptions just like adults when they are under stress. It is more common in children who have experienced traumatic events. Also, the family can cause stress to the child, leading to them experiencing more night waking. These sleep interruptions are closely associated with high-stress hormonal levels.

- *Hunger*: Even in adults, sleeping on an empty stomach can be a nuisance. Your baby should be fed shortly before bedtime to avoid having to feed a sleepy child who might not feed well and then go to bed hungry. Feeding should take place one hour before sleeping so that it helps the baby to avoid feeling uncomfortable when sleeping on a full stomach. Children who sleep when hungry can develop health complications apart from sleep complications.

- *Thirst*: Your child may be dehydrated after all the activities of the day. Encourage them to take lots of water before bedtime to reduce the chances of them waking up in the middle of the night through thirst. However, they should not drink just before bedtime, because your baby might need to urinate in the middle of the night. Make it a habit for children to rehydrate during the day, and set a drinking time well before bedtime that will not interfere with their sleep.

- *Noise*: Just as noise can interfere with an adult's sleep, so can it for children. To avoid this menace, especially when you are living in a noisy neighbourhood, try using a white-noise generator or hanging heavy curtains that will reduce the noise from outside. Your child's room should be left undisturbed, because even opening their door may wake them up.

- *Full or irritable bladders*: Most children may drift away from their sleep at night because of their urge to urinate. It is wise for parents not to give their children drinks right before bedtime. Children with urinary tract problem may wake up during the night without necessarily their bladders being full. It is more common in girls due to the infections as their urethra is very short; making it easy for germs and other

15

micro-orgasms to enter the body. If a baby has developed a UTI it is important to visit a physician who will provide antibiotics for the problem.

- *Overtiredness*: The child's body functions in other ways similar to that of an adult. When children are exhausted past their limits, their sleep might become more restless, and they might experience more night waking. Children who experience this problem need more sleep and, therefore, their bedtime routine should be adjusted to accommodate more sleep time.

2.2 Sleep Disorders

Infants and children may experience sleep disorders. Short or poor-quality sleep is associated with a wide array of problems in children, including health, academic, behavioural and developmental problems.

Your child may experience difficulties in falling or staying asleep when they suffer from one or more sleep disorders. Developments in childhood play a vital role in paediatric sleep. Some of these paediatric sleep disorders include:

Sleeplessness in infants

This is the most common form of sleep disorder in children. It can be managed easily when the actual cause is determined. The most efficient way to prevent your child from developing sleep disorder is to introduce consistent bedtime routines during the early stages of infancy. Young infants do not know the difference between day and night, and thus depend on the parent to create their sleep patterns. When infants develop sleeplessness, it is important to identify the cause, as infants tend to sleep more because of the growth that is taking place in their bodies.

You should teach your children independence from an early age by letting them sleep in their own bed without you being present. This will help your child drift back to sleep easily after normal night waking. Independent and self-soothing children are associated with extended and healthier sleep compared to those whose parents have to play an active role in making them fall asleep. Independence is crucial, as it lasts throughout childhood if developed at an early age.

Arousal disorders

This is a common disorder in toddlers and adolescent children. It is an episode that transitions your child from deep sleep to partially awake or very light sleep; your child exhibits features that can be translated as them being awake. They normally seem confused and disoriented during this transition period and can be unresponsive to any stimulation from you or environmental changes. Normally, your child will not remember anything that occurred during the episode.

Your child can only experience one episode a night, and it usually occurs within the first two hours of falling asleep. However, there are exceptional cases where they might experience more than one episode on the same night but then go for a couple of weeks without experiencing it again. Possible triggers for these episodes may include travel, health problems, irregular sleep and waking schedules, and abrupt sleep loss. Genetics play a crucial role in this case, and it has been discovered that more than 60% of children who suffer from arousal disorders come from a family with a history of this disorder.

Epidemiology

At some point, almost 40% of children experience sleep disorders considered to be significant to their parents. Children with serious physical illness such as asthma and psychiatric problems such as attention deficit are particularly prone to sleep disorders. It is important for these children to take their medication at the proper time to avoid complicating their sleep further.

Serious conditions such as asthma require parents to sacrifice their sleep at least once or twice every night to go and check the child.

Parasomnias

There are several forms of parasomnias which may occur as primary sleep phenomena or other forms related to psychiatric problems or physical illness. Most of these gradually resolve with time, and you should reassure your children by explaining this to them. You should also take safety measures to avoid injuries to the child in cases where your child sleep walks. Parasomnias manifest in a wide spectrum of conditions such as nightmares, arousal syndrome, as well as night terrors. Genetics play a role in this condition, so it is important to give your child all the support they need during this phase. From the age of ten, the conditions associated with this disorder reduce and completely phase out in most the children. When your child is showing some of the symptoms of this disorder, it is important to make them feel safe and to physically make their rooms safe. It is also important to keep lines of communication open and to continue reassuring them.

Obstructive sleep apnoea (OSA)

This is a condition that occurs when the airway partially or totally collapses continuously throughout the night; the soft throat tissues relax, blocking the airway and disrupting sleep-associated breathing. This resultant drop in oxygen level in the body causes your child to wake up for some time until their breathing returns to normal. Sleep Apnoea is not a usual occurrence among children and can be difficult to recognise at first.

Noisy breathing and snoring are not normal in children. OSA in children is mostly ignored because the symptoms are very different from those in adults. Children with medical conditions that affect their facial structure, neuromuscular system, or nose and airway are more prone to developing OSA. Parents with children that suffer from Down's syndrome ought to be very aware of the high risk and take their children for evaluation in instances of a behavioural change that may lead to or be related to OSA. Common symptoms of OSA in children include snoring, enlarged adenoids and tonsils, mouth breathing, bed wetting and excessive daytime sleepiness.

2.3 Triggers for Sleep Problems

Dummies: The most common trigger for sleep problems is the dummy. They cause 90% of all sleep problems in children under 18 months old. There are three main reasons why a baby with a dummy wakes more frequently than one without:

- A baby with a dummy seems to find it harder to achieve deep sleep; their intermittent sucking seems to disturb their sleep pattern.

- A baby who goes to sleep with a dummy will wake up expecting to suck, but if the dummy has fallen out, the baby will shout out for you to come and put it in again. Unfortunately, by the time you decide to go in and replace the dummy, your baby is so awake that it is harder for them to get back to sleep, even when you have replaced the dummy.

- The constant sucking on the dummy tricks the body into thinking there is food coming, which causes them to digest their milk too fast and makes them hungrier than a baby without a dummy.

Rocking your baby to sleep: This is an action that you should avoid letting your child depend on. This means that when your baby wakes during their sleep cycle transitions, they will need you to rock them back to sleep. As the baby grows, the duration of rocking required will also increase.

Feeding a baby to slumber: Most mothers sooth their baby through breast feeding or giving them a bottle. The child then gets used to suckling to sleep. This makes it harder for another person to get your child back to sleep.

Moving house: It is common in modern society for families to relocate from one house to another. New environments can also trigger sleeping problems. It is therefore important to make sure that the child sleeps in the same bed they are used to in the new house.

2.4 Solutions to Sleep Disorders

Sleep disorders are rarely recognised by general practitioners. Before a treatment is initiated, it is important to establish the nature and development of the sleep disorder. The sleeping environment of your child and their activities may have an adverse effect on the child's sleeping patterns. Polysomnography is the gold standard for children with sleep-associated breathing problems.

Obstructive sleep apnoea treatment may include non-surgical treatment of continuous positive airway pressure, nasal resistors, positional therapy, oropharyngeal exercises and the use of oral appliances. Also, behavioural adjustments may be made to help with the treatment. Where these methods cannot help, practitioners resort to surgery, but this is mostly used only in severe cases.

Restless sleep can be treated through a combination of behavioural adjustments and pharmacological treatments. Supplements of vitamins and iron may be offered to your child, as limb movement disorder is sometimes a result of iron or vitamin deficiency. If the condition is severe, drug treatment may be used.

Insomnia is treated both with non-pharmacological and medication processes. Cognitive behavioural therapy is used to treat different psychological conditions and other conditions that do not need medication. Medication treatment can be used in children who have reached a severe stage. There are many insomnia medications on the market and, if used inappropriately, they can cause severe side effects.

The brain's inability to control sleep–wake routines can result in a chronic sleep disorder known as narcolepsy. Treatment involves medication, scheduled short naps and improving the quality of bedtime sleep. This is like training your child's brain to control its sleep routines.

Nightmares have no medical treatment. However, parents can use things that will reassure their children of their security, such as favourite stuffed toys and bedding. The parent should also listen to the child if there is something disturbing them.

Sleep paralysis can be treated through a thorough and fixed routine of rest, meals and recreation. It is a temporary phenomenon that will not require medical treatment.

2.5 Where Should Your Baby Sleep?

We are warned about sleeping with our children in the same bed, in their rooms, on a couch and many other things. The truth of the matter is that a baby can sleep in so many places; this is because your child is human and has their own preferences. You just have to learn what your child's preference is. A child will sleep better in an environment in which they are more comfortable. However, it is your duty as a parent to make your child comfortable in their own bed.

Co-sleeping refers to common sleep in the marital bed. Most parents fear co-sleeping because it can make their children spoilt and dependent. But it also has its advantages. Your baby drifts into REM sleep after a certain period, depending on their age. During these transitions your baby is more likely to wake, but they will sleep easily when they feel they are secure, and that is brought about by having someone near them. For the first month, your child can sleep with you to get comfort and reassurance.

As your child grows, you should be able to encourage independence in their life. The first area in which to teach a child independence is sleeping patterns and habits. Research shows that children who have independent sleeping routines end up building strong and confident personalities. To start, make your children sleep in their own beds. This can pose a challenge because not many children will readily accept sleeping alone. Here are some tips to persuade your child to sleep in their own bed:

- Start teaching your child early how to sleep in their own bed. It will be hard to change a routine that the child is already used to. To avoid this, start a routine that will not require any

- major changes. Children are very adaptive, but they can also be manipulative. They will cry the first day they are left to sleep alone but adapt in no time if you do not give in to their manipulation.

- Reconfigure bedtime. Most children fear the unknown when they are left to sleep independently. Stay with your child in their room and gradually withdraw your presence

- from their environment. Instead of sleeping with your child on your bed then later carrying them to their beds, sit with them on their beds until they fall asleep. After a few days, switch to sitting on a chair while they are in bed and slowly move the chair away from them till they get used to sleeping alone.

- Be consistent with the routine. Do not cave in for special circumstances that your child may invent. When its bedtime, make sure everyone goes to their beds. This will automatically register in their brain that at bedtime they are supposed to go to their beds. This is easier, because children associate sleep with other external factors such as beds, bottles or simply soothing them.

- Make it worthwhile. Encourage your child by rewarding them for sleeping in their own bed; for instance, give them extra play time or offer them sticker charts. This will motivate them to sleep in their own beds, because they want the rewards. Also, make it fun by reading a storybook or poem to them, or just have a quiet time to talk to them.

- Create a plan of action. Making your child go to their bed may be easier than making them stay in their beds. Create something that will make them stay in their beds if they wake up. Give them something comforting and fun to think about; this will also help them drift back to sleep without unnecessarily waking you up.

CHAPTER 3

3.1 Baby Sleep Tricks

Your baby can be a bundle of joy, but what you never anticipate is that they can give you another non-payable job during bedtime. Night-time screams and cries can be really exhausting, especially when you have had a long day in your paying job. Here are some tricks that are easy to follow that will make your child continue being a bundle of joy.

Take away the pacifier at bedtime

Normally, your infant's reflexes and motor actions are not well established, and they will scream when they lose their soothers. Although experts state that the use of pacifiers during bedtime reduces the chances of sudden infancy death syndrome (SIDS), your child will throw tantrums in their bed until you wake up and return their pacifiers. It can be really hard for the first few days hearing your child cry for their soother, but they will get used to sleeping without it, and you will return to having peaceful nights. Instead, you can replace their pacifiers with their thumb. This will sooth your child to sleep, as many infants are still at the oral stage and are soothed by having things in their mouths.

Play white-noise sounds

Your baby can be woken up by noise from outside, especially when you live in a noisy neighbourhood or you have a noisy neighbour. Use a fan or white-noise gadgets to generate the soft noise that will prevent your baby from focusing on the outside noise. Make it a routine to switch it on during bedtime for them; it may also work as a soother to send them back to sleep when they experience normal night waking. White noise can even be downloaded from an online platform to your MP3 player.

Avoid soothing the baby for long

Babies are curious creatures, and when they reach a new developmental stage such as learning how to crawl, they will be so excited about practising their new development that it will sometimes exceed their bedtime. Be strict on the bedtime and wake-up routine so that they do not interfere with yours. If you entertain them way past their bedtime, that will be the new routine.

Stop night-time feeding

Your baby will get used to going back to sleep without nursing. Once your paediatrician has given you the green light to do away with night-time feeding, it's the time to train them. If your baby is used to feeding in the middle of the night, be prepared to wake up when they start crying. Make sure your baby is well fed before bedtime, but also not overfed, to prevent them from waking up at night due to hunger.

3.2 How to Get Your Child to Sleep Throughout the Night

Some children are capable of sleeping throughout the night at six weeks, but the majority are not until the age of 4–6 months. At this age, your baby has the capability to sleep for more than eight hours uninterrupted and drift back to sleep after normal night waking. Your

child should be trained to develop healthy sleeping habits from as early as five months.

Scheduled awakening

The idea is to alter your child's sleeping behaviour by waking them up before they actually wake up. You should observe your child's sleeping pattern, then change it. For instance, if the child wakes up at 1 a.m. and 5 a.m., wake them up 15 minutes before their usual time and rock them or sooth them back to sleep. Then adjust the waking time to 1:15 a.m. and 5:15 a.m. Then continue adjusting the time until they do not wake up before you wake them up. As you make this a routine, your baby will eventually learn to sleep throughout the night. Although this approach takes longer than other methods, it is better for children who have defined waking times.

Ferberizing

This approach is based on the idea that your children make associations with falling asleep. When you or a caregiver rocks the child or soothes them in any way to sleep, the child associates that act with sleep. Children then become dependent on these things, and they will want them repeated each time they wake up during the night. The trick is to make your child learn how to fall asleep by themselves in their beds.

This is how this approach works:

Once your baby is in their bed, leave their room. When they start crying, give yourself an allowance of five minutes before you go in to comfort them, but without picking them up from their bed. When they cry again, adjust your allowance to 10 minutes before you go into soothe them. Keep adding five minutes to your allowance until they fall asleep. The point of going in to soothe your baby is to reassure them that they are fine. This routine should be repeated every night, and a specific time set as their bedtime.

The allowance that you begin with should gradually increase as days go by. For instance, on the first day you gave them an allowance of five minutes before going to check on them, now give them 10 minutes, then 15 minutes on the third day. This method is effective, as your baby learns to associate their bed with sleep and also removes the notion that crying will make you pick them up. Within a week, they will be able to sleep for longer uninterrupted hours. However, this method is not popular, as not many parents will allow their infants to cry for longer without being taken care of.

Reinforce sleep rhythms

This approach is based on parents monitoring their child so that they do not become overtired, as when your baby is too fatigued it will cause them sleeping problems. The parents anticipate their infants sleeping time then send them for naps or to bed.

This is how the approach works:

When your child is about four months old, keep their intervals of waking brief, between one and two hours, then lay them down for a nap. Older infants can take 2–3 naps a day, as they can handle the pressure of being awake. This approach requires you to be keen and anticipate when your child will be sleepy.

Schedule an early bedtime routine. The appropriate time to set bedtime is between 6 p.m. and 8 p.m., depending on their daytime nap schedule. Children who have a late bedtime routine experience problems falling or staying asleep.

The family bed

This is when your child shares a bed with you and is common in many cultures as part of child rearing. This method is good, as it strengthens the bond between you and your child. This is considered to be more of a sleeping routine than a technique to help your child sleep throughout the night. It gives them a sense of security, and also the mother does not have to wake up at regular intervals to go and check on their baby. However, this method is not the best, as apart

31

from saying goodbye to privacy, there is a high chance of the parent rolling over the child. It also hinders your child from developing the sense of independence that is brought about by them sleeping alone.

3.3 Safe Sleep Guidelines

You should make sure your baby's crib meets safety standards before purchasing it. Your baby's crib should have a firm mattress with tight fitting sheets. All the stuffed toys, pillows, bumpers and other cute accessories that are placed in their crib often do more harm to your baby than good. They should be cleared during nap times and bedtime.

Also, avoid placing your baby's crib near windows or walls that have decorative accessories hanging on them. This is to avoid anything falling on your child during sleep. It is safer for you to share a room with your child than share a bed with them. Keep the bed close for necessary observation, and return your baby to their crib after the night feeding.

Babies should be laid on their backs during a nap and at bedtime to reduce the incidence of sudden infant death syndrome (SIDS). You should also instruct the person you are allowing to look after your child on how to put your child to rest. Always make sure that, when you cover your baby during sleep, their head is not covered. Use sleep sacks rather than the usual blankets to avoid your baby pulling them during sleep and suffocating.

As parents with a newborn, you will need to learn how to perform CPR in case of an emergency. This will reduce the panic that most parents go through when something happens to their baby. Do not place your baby for sleep on the sofa or on your bed if they are able to roll.

Reduce your child's exposure to smoke, because smoke increases the risk of sudden infant death syndrome. If the mother smokes, she should smoke after feeding their baby, not before. Keep the house and car smoke free for the safety of your child.

CHAPTER 4

Sleep needs, problems and habits are different in different children. Sometimes we try to compare our child's sleeping patterns to those of our friend's, neighbour's or relative's child. We become excessively worried when our children's sleeping patterns are different from those of people's around us. In this chapter, we will focus on FAQs and sleeping schedules for our children.

4.1 *FAQs*

Here are some questions that we are asked and answers to some of them.

- Why does my newborn stay up all night and sleep all day?

This is a common question, especially from new parents. Your child is very sleepy during the day, but immediately it is dark they become very active. This is a normal phenomenon during your child's early stages, especially when they are between 4–6 weeks old. During this period, your child does not know the difference between day and night. It will help if you encourage your child make the distinction between day and night so they can assume normal sleeping hours. This can be done by making the house brighter and active during the day, and dark and quiet during the night. However, during their early stages, you may also adapt to your child's sleeping patterns and sleep during the day to avoid fatigue.

- How much sleep does my newborn need?

The sleeping patterns of your child will gradually change as they grow up. This means they will need different amounts of sleep at certain stages of their growth. Here is an outline to help you determine the amount of sleep your child needs at a certain stage.

0–3 months old: 14–17 hours per day

4–11 months old: 12–15 hours per day

1–2 years old: 11–14 hours per day

3–5 years old: 10–13 hours per day

6–13 years old: 9–11 hours per day

The right amount of sleep is essential for your child to be energetic, refreshed and happy. Sometimes, when the child is not getting the right amount and quality of sleep, you are not getting it either. This sleep loss has been closely associated to postpartum depression and weight gain in first-time mothers.

- How can I tell that my baby is getting tired?

Most new parents have an issue knowing when their children are tired, and they wait until they are overtired to put them to bed. This is a problem, as we discussed earlier in the book, because an overtired child will not sleep well. Here are some signs that your child is tired.

➢ rubbing eyes
➢ pulling ears
➢ yawning
➢ arching back

When you see your child showing these signs, it's time for bed or a nap.

- How many naps should my baby have in a day?

It all depends on the age of your child, and you should know that children are different. It is not necessarily true that your child will sleep for the same duration as their peers, but here are some healthy guidelines.

0–3 months old: 4–5 naps per day

3–6 months old: 3 naps per day

6–14 months old: 2 naps per day

15 months–3 years old: 1 nap per day

Each of the naps should last for about 1–3 hours.

- How can I get my child to sleep for longer?

This is a common question from first-time parents. Your child will sleep for longer if they have learned to fall asleep independently. This means the child is able to drift back to sleep when they wake. A standard sleep cycle lasts up to 45 minutes at a time in both your children and you. So if your child cannot sleep by themselves, you might have to wake up after their sleep cycle.

- Is it normal for my baby to snore?

Snoring may be a result of a blocked nose or a cold. However, if it happens regularly, even when the child is completely healthy, it may be a sign of obstructive sleep apnoea (OSA). This is a condition that blocks your child's upper airway, stopping them from breathing during sleep. It also interferes with your child's sleeping hours, as they cannot sleep for longer. This may require treatment or medication.

- What can I do to stop my child from resisting bedtimes?

Make exercise a daily habit. This will wear out your child, making them want to go to bed at the end of the day without being asked. Keep bedtime consistent. As children grow, their sleeping patterns change. You should monitor your child to learn their sleeping patterns and arrange bedtime according to those patterns. Some of the resistance is brought about just to catch your attention. Spend time with your child before bedtime to reduce the resistance.

Maintain a fair, regular nap time. If your child sleeps until late in the evening, the chance that they will not be sleepy by bedtime is high. Give them a short nap time, and if they want more, they will have to wait for bedtime.

4.2 Sleeping Schedules

Sleep is important to your child, because it has a direct effect on their mental and physical development. A child who has had a proper sleep is usually energetic and playful afterwards. Your child spends much of their childhood, approximately 40%, sleeping.

There are two states of sleep:

Non-rapid eye movements (NREM): during this state of sleep, energy is restored, hormones responsible for growth and development are released, there is an occurrence of tissue repair and growth, and the blood supply to the muscles is increased.

Rapid eye movement: it is during this state that dreams occur and our brains are active. Body movement, breathing and heart rates become irregular.

Children spend 50% of their time in each state, and the estimated sleep cycle is about 50 minutes. When your child is around six months old, their sleep will be compromised of 30% REM sleep. At around their preschool age, your child's sleep cycle will be about 90 minutes.

- **Newborns (0–3 months)**

Sleep during this stage occurs frequently, and sleep–wake cycles are associated with your baby's need to have their nappy changed, and be fed and nurtured. Your baby will probably sleep between 16–18 hours a day, with a period of between one and three hours spent awake in between sleeps. At this stage your baby will sleep in two- to four-hour intervals and wake up to eat.

They tend to stir and look restless during their sleep because of reflexes they can't control.

Total Sleep: 16–18 hours
Night-time Sleep: 8–9 hours
Naps: 7–9 hours (3–5 naps)

- **Infants (4–11 months)**

At this stage, night feedings will mostly not be necessary, and your child will probably sleep throughout the night. However, most children do this at nine months old. Your baby will possibly sleep about 9–12 hours during the night. You should create an enjoyable and consistent bedtime routine, regular daytime and bedtime schedules, and encourage them to sleep independently.

Total Sleep: 14–15 hours
Night-time Sleep: 10–11 hours
Naps: 4–5 hours (2–3 naps)

- **Toddlers (1–2 years)**

Your child will need about 11–14 hours of sleep a day. Naptimes decrease as they grow up, lasting about 1–3 hours. Daytime naps should not be scheduled close to bedtime, as your child will have trouble sleeping. It is at this stage that your child will exhibit more sleep-related problems. Their sleep may be affected by the increase in their cognitive, motor and social abilities.

Total Sleep: 11–14 hours
Night-time Sleep: 10–11 hours
Naps: 1–3 hours (1–2 naps)

- **Pre-schoolers (3–5 years)**

Your child will normally sleep for 11–13 hours each night, and their nap time will almost be null. Sleep-related problems may increase due to development of imagination. At this stage, try to make sure the sleeping environment is the same for your child each night. Try to control their use of media so that they can sleep.

Total Sleep: 11–13 hours
Night-time Sleep: 10–11 hours
Naps: 1–2 hours (0–1 naps)

- **School-aged Children (6–13 years)**

Your child will probably need to sleep for 9–11 hours. Sleep-related problems will intensify because of the increase in daily activity. Sleep disorders and problems are more common at this stage.

Total Sleep: 10–11 hours
Night-time Sleep: 10–11 hours
Naps: 0

CONCLUSION

The "Off Button" varies from child to child; the secret is knowing which one belongs to your child. You may use more than one technique to get your child to sleep throughout the night. If none of them work, you should consider taking your child to a paediatrician to be examined for sleep disorders. Consistency will give you the best results, as most approaches are not easy. Some of the issues that make your child wake up in the middle of the night are a result of routines you have forced them to get used to. Start by slowly bringing in new routines that will enable both of you to sleep through the night.

CPSIA information can be obtained
at www.ICGtesting.com
Printed in the USA
LVHW051524110522
718483LV00009B/464